Simple Salvation

Darlene Palmer

Copyright © 2021. Darlene Palmer and Palmer's Notepad. All rights reserved.

This book or any portion thereof may not be reproduced or used in any manner whatsoever without the express written permission of the author and publisher except for the use of brief quotations in a book review.

Scriptures taken from the KING JAMES VERSION (KJV): KING JAMES VERSION, are public domain.

"Scriptures quoted from (NLT) are taken from the Holy Bible, New Living Translation, copyright © 1996, 2004, 2007 by Tyndale House Foundation. Used by permission of Tyndale House Publishers, Inc., Carol Stream, IL 60188. All rights reserved."

Printed in the United States of America.

ISBN: 978-1-7378268-0-4

Moreno Valley, CA

For those who seek a Savior.

*For Everyone
who calls on the name of
the L ORD will be saved*
(Romans 10:13).

Table of Contents

Introduction 15
Simple Salvation 19
A New Birth 23
A New Family 27
A New Truth 31
A New Mind 35
A New Location 41
A New Destination 47
The Decision 51
Steps To Grow 57
A Prayer Plan 61
   ADORATION 62
   COMMUNICATE 63

SILENCE 64
GRATITUDE 65
Conclusion........................ 67
Darlene Palmer................ 75

Simple Salvation

Have you ever wondered what it *really* means to be saved?

Have you ever wondered how to effectively change your life for the better?

Have you ever wondered where you will go when you die?

The answers *to these questions and more are* ***inside!***

Acknowledgments

All praise be to God. Every bit of acknowledgment and all thanks belong to God the Father and His Son, Jesus Christ. Without their saving grace in my life, none of this would be possible.

Darlene Palmer's Simple Salvation

Introduction

Receiving Jesus Christ as Lord and Savior is the simplest yet most life-changing decision we could ever make.

Unfortunately, people have been made to think the process of salvation or being born-again is confusing and

Darlene Palmer's Simple Salvation

difficult. This is far from the truth.

This small pocketbook explains what it means to be saved, outlines the plan of salvation, and presents an opportunity to be saved. It is a beginner's guide to new life as a Christian.

Simple Salvation is an excellent introduction to the Gospel Message, perfect for every new believer and those

Darlene Palmer's Simple Salvation

considering a decision for Christ.

Darlene Palmer's Simple Salvation

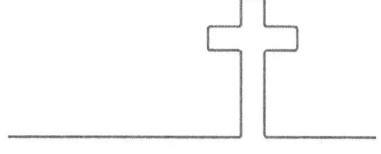

Darlene Palmer's Simple Salvation

Simple Salvation

Salvation comes from believing. Believing God loved us so much that He gave the life of His Son to take away our sins so that we could have eternal life.

Salvation is a gift from God and is received only by faith.

Darlene Palmer's Simple Salvation

God saved you by his grace when you believed. And you can't take credit for this; it is a gift from God (Ephesians 2:8).

Salvation comes through belief in one man only, Jesus Christ.

There is salvation in no one else! God has given no other name under heaven by which we must be saved (Acts 4:12).

Darlene Palmer's Simple Salvation

With salvation comes a new way of living.

This means that anyone who belongs to Christ has become a new person. The old life is gone; a new life has begun (2 Corinthians 5:17)!

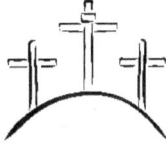

Darlene Palmer's Simple Salvation

Darlene Palmer's Simple Salvation

A New Birth

Once a person accepts the free gift of salvation, they become **spiritually born again, and their new life has begun.**

> *Jesus replied, "I tell you the truth, unless you are born again, you cannot see the Kingdom of God"*
> *(John 3:3).*

Darlene Palmer's Simple Salvation

God made everyone with three parts: spirit, mind, and body. It is our spirit that is ***born again***. It is made new.

It is also with our spirit that we communicate with God, and with our spirit, we worship Him as Lord.

For God is Spirit, so those who worship Him must worship in spirit and in truth (John 4:24).

Darlene Palmer's Simple Salvation

Our soul then begins to be renewed and directed by the words of God in the Bible. And our body learns to cooperate with our born-again spirit and our renewed mind.

Darlene Palmer's Simple Salvation

*Put on your new nature,
created to be like God – truly
righteous and holy
(Ephesians 4:24).*

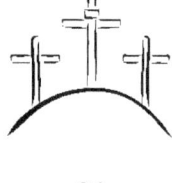

Darlene Palmer's Simple Salvation

A New Family

Being born again is like a child being born into a family and for whatever reason, the child is removed and placed into another family.

Usually, the new family has better means to care for the child and often changes the child's name. You could say the child is born again. The same thing happens regarding salvation.

When we make the decision to become born again, we are removed from the devil's family of sin and placed into God's family of righteousness.

God now becomes your Father. You become His child. You even get a new name: Christian.

Darlene Palmer's Simple Salvation

Even before he made the world, God loved us and chose us in Christ to be holy and without fault in his eyes. God decided in advance to adopt us into his own family by bringing us to himself through Jesus Christ. This is what he wanted to do, and it gave him great pleasure (Ephesians 1:4-5).

Darlene Palmer's Simple Salvation

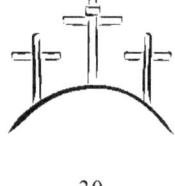

Darlene Palmer's Simple Salvation

A New Truth

The truth is the devil hates losing. His plan is for you to remain unsaved, which will seal your membership into his family the moment you die. The Bible warns us not to be deceived by him.

Darlene Palmer's Simple Salvation

*Dear children,
don't let anyone deceive you
about this: When people do
what is right, it shows that they
are righteous, even as Christ is
righteous. But when people
keep on sinning, it shows
that they belong to the devil
(1 John 3:7-8).*

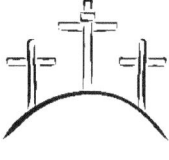

Darlene Palmer's Simple Salvation

We must understand that **the devil is the enemy of God and the enemy of man.** He is the opposite of everything that God is. God is good; the devil is evil. God is truth; the devil is a liar. God is light; the devil is darkness.

There is a clear difference between Father God and the devil. There is also a difference between the children of God and the children of the devil.

Darlene Palmer's Simple Salvation

We must decide to which family we will belong. **We cannot belong to both God's family and the devil's family.**

> *So now we can tell who are children of God and who are children of the devil. Anyone who does not live righteously and does not love other believers does not belong to God*
> *(1 John 3:10).*

A New Mind

The Christian's mind and way of thinking needs to change after salvation.

Rather than listening to the thoughts of the devil and being influenced by the world, a Christian must begin to think like Jesus and become more Christ-minded.

Jesus was constantly thinking of His fellow man. So, He left us with the following instructions:

Darlene Palmer's Simple Salvation

Then make me truly happy by agreeing wholeheartedly with each other, loving one another, and working together with one mind and purpose. Don't be selfish; don't try to impress others. Be humble, thinking of others as better than yourselves. Don't look out only for your own interests, but take an interest in others, too (Philippians 2:2-4).

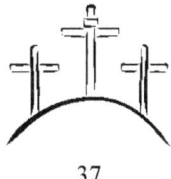

Darlene Palmer's Simple Salvation

As you read the Bible daily, you will find basic instructions for living a successful Christian life.

The Bible must become the most important and the most frequently read book in your life.

The more you read, the more you begin to think and act like Jesus.

Darlene Palmer's Simple Salvation

Study this Book of Instruction daily. Meditate on it day and night so you will be sure to obey everything written in it. Only then will you prosper and succeed in all you do (Joshua 1:8).

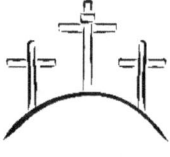

Darlene Palmer's Simple Salvation

Darlene Palmer's Simple Salvation

A New Location

Believers are to separate themselves as much as possible from all forms of darkness.

Sometimes it may mean changing your friends and those with whom you keep company. It may even mean changing your physical

Darlene Palmer's Simple Salvation

location.

> *Therefore, come out from among unbelievers, and separate yourselves from them, says the LORD. Don't touch their filthy things, and I will welcome you*
> *(2 Corinthians 6:17).*

When you begin to fellowship in the light, you will find new friends who are saved like you. Friends who will encourage you in your

Darlene Palmer's Simple Salvation

Christian walk.

> *But if we walk in the light as He is in the light, we have fellowship with one another, and the blood of Jesus Christ His Son cleanses us from all sin (1 John 1:7).*

Jesus is in the light. Therefore, we must be in the light also. Jesus was careful who He fellowshipped with, and He was careful where He went. Yes, Jesus did hang out in some dark places with sinners when He wanted to expose their sin and bring light and salvation to their situations.

As Christians, we must follow Christ's example and **stay away from places where darkness gathers unless you are there to expose the sin by bringing in Christ and His salvation.**

Darlene Palmer's Simple Salvation

*But their evil intentions will be
exposed when the light shines
on them, for the light makes
everything visible
(Ephesians 5:13-14).*

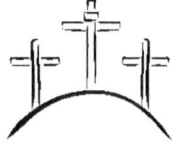

Darlene Palmer's Simple Salvation

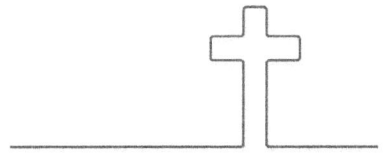

Darlene Palmer's Simple Salvation

A New Destination

Finally, the Bible answers a major question on the minds of people everywhere: **When I die, will I go to heaven?**

The answer for the true born-again believer is, **yes, you will go to heaven.** It is guaranteed.

Darlene Palmer's Simple Salvation

*Yes, we are fully confident,
and we would rather be away
from these earthly bodies,
for then we will be at home
with the Lord
(2 Corinthians 5:8).*

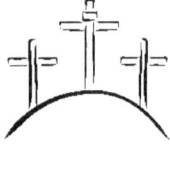

Darlene Palmer's Simple Salvation

The Lord's home is heaven, and immediately after death, Christians are welcomed into heaven. A place in the Father's house has already been prepared for those who love Him.

> *When everything is ready,*
> *I will come and get you,*
> *so that you will always*
> *be with me where I am*
> *(John 14:3).*

Darlene Palmer's Simple Salvation

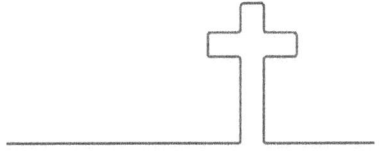

Darlene Palmer's Simple Salvation

The Decision

Now you know what it means to be saved and understand the wonderful changes that salvation brings to your life. It is time to make the decision to accept Jesus Christ into your heart as your Lord and Savior.

Darlene Palmer's Simple Salvation

The way of salvation is simple, and the instruction is clear:

If you confess with your mouth that Jesus is Lord and believe in your heart that God raised him from the dead, you will be saved. For it is by believing in your heart that you are made right with God, and it is by confessing with your mouth that you are saved (Romans 10:9-10).

Darlene Palmer's Simple Salvation

Pray the following prayer with your whole heart, and you will be saved:

Darlene Palmer's Simple Salvation

Father God,

I believe Jesus Christ is Your Son and that He came into the world to save me from sin. I believe that He died for me and that He was raised from the dead.

I accept the salvation that You have provided for me through Jesus.

Jesus, I give You my life.

I ask You to forgive all of my

Darlene Palmer's Simple Salvation

*sins, and I confess that You
are my Personal Savior.*

Be Lord over my life.

*Thank You, God,
for saving me!*

In Jesus' name.

Amen.

Darlene Palmer's Simple Salvation

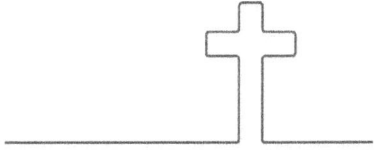

Darlene Palmer's Simple Salvation

Steps To Grow

Congratulations, you have accepted Jesus into your heart and life. ***You are now "Saved!"***

Your next step is to develop a simple daily plan to help you grow in your new life as a Christian. Use the following steps to guide you:

Darlene Palmer's Simple Salvation

STEP 1: FELLOWSHIP

Attend and join a Bible-based church:

A bible-based church teaches from the Bible.

Darlene Palmer's Simple Salvation

STEP 2: READ

Read your Bible daily:

Read the Bible every day. Do not get discouraged if you do not understand what you read. Understanding will come in time. Ask God to give you a mentor, someone who has been a Christian longer than you. Someone to help you learn and encourage you in your Christian walk.

Darlene Palmer's Simple Salvation

STEP 3: PRAY

Have a talk with God.

On the following pages is a simple 20-minute prayer plan.

Darlene Palmer's Simple Salvation

A Prayer Plan

Darlene Palmer's Simple Salvation

ADORATION

Worship for 5 minutes

Spend five minutes telling God that you love Him and how wonderful He is. Sing songs that praise and glorify Him.

Darlene Palmer's Simple Salvation

COMMUNICATE

Talk for 5 minutes

Spend five minutes talking to God about what's on your heart. Then, speak to Him about what you read in the Bible. You can also make requests.

Darlene Palmer's Simple Salvation

SILENCE

Be quiet for 5 minutes

Spend five minutes taking time to listen for God. He wants to talk to you. So be still, sit quietly, and write down anything you hear.

Darlene Palmer's Simple Salvation

GRATITUDE

Be thankful for 5 minutes

Thank God and praise Him for what He has done in your life.

Darlene Palmer's Simple Salvation

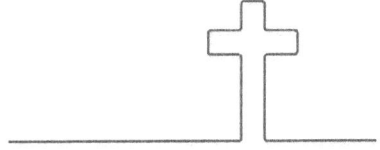

Conclusion

Jesus Christ, the Son of God, came to earth to save us all from sin. Sin came into the world through Adam and Eve, the ancestral parents of all mankind. Therefore, sin is automatically a part of our lives.

Darlene Palmer's Simple Salvation

We are born as sinners, in need of a Savior.

Darlene Palmer's Simple Salvation

*Because one person disobeyed
God, many became sinners.
But because one other person
obeyed God, many
will be made righteous
(Roman 5:19).*

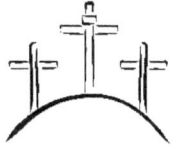

Darlene Palmer's Simple Salvation

One man, Adam, disobeyed God and brought the nature of sin into the world. One man, Jesus Christ, obeyed God and destroyed sin by his death on the cross for all who will believe in Him.

The Father God loved the world so much that He sacrificed the life of His only Son, Jesus Christ, to save us from sin and call us righteous.

Darlene Palmer's Simple Salvation

*For God loved the world
so much that He gave His one
and only Son, so that everyone
who believes in Him will not
perish but have eternal life
(John 3:16).*

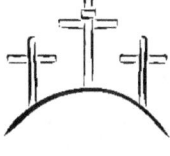

Darlene Palmer's Simple Salvation

Darlene Palmer's Simple Salvation

From The Author's Heart

Simple Salvation was written in a simple format that all can read and understand in hopes of bringing many souls to Christ in this End-time Harvest.

Darlene Palmer's Simple Salvation

Darlene Palmer

A former Case Manager, Darlene Palmer, worked with and touched the lives of people of every age, ethnicity, and social-economic background for more than fifteen years.

Her passion is for all to be saved and to come to the knowledge of the truth

(1 Timothy 2:4). That passion ignited a burning desire in her to find a simple way to spread the Gospel of Christ and a simple, easy-to-understand method for all to become saved.

You may contact the author via email at:

palmersnotepad@gmail.com

Palmer's notepad

www.ingramcontent.com/pod-product-compliance
Lightning Source LLC
Chambersburg PA
CBHW062150100526
44589CB00014B/1774